Psychological Trauma
and PTSD/Soldiers
(Child)

Psychological Trauma and PTSD/Soldiers (Child)

ELIAS RINALDO GAMBORIKO,
A.J., PH.D.

authorHOUSE®

AuthorHouse™
1663 Liberty Drive
Bloomington, IN 47403
www.authorhouse.com
Phone: 1-800-839-8640

First published by AuthorHouse   01/23/2012

ISBN: 978-1-4685-4711-5 (sc)
ISBN: 978-1-4685-4712-2 (ebk)

Library of Congress Control Number: 2012901359

Printed in the United States of America

Any people depicted in stock imagery provided by Thinkstock are models, and such images are being used for illustrative purposes only.
Certain stock imagery © Thinkstock.

This book is printed on acid-free paper.

Because of the dynamic nature of the Internet, any web addresses or links contained in this book may have changed since publication and may no longer be valid. The views expressed in this work are solely those of the author and do not necessarily reflect the views of the publisher, and the publisher hereby disclaims any responsibility for them.

"Most evidence suggests that ordinary children, faced with the extraordinary circumstances of combat, are capable of learning to kill and to kill repeatedly." Fall 2008 Issue

—Michael Wessells,
Child Soldiers: From Violence to Protection

When you think of war, what images come to mind? Perhaps you see rows of uniformed soldiers marching in step, or tanks and armored vehicles traveling in convoy, or the U.S. military's televised "Shock and Awe" precision bombings over Iraq. The reality, however, is that the majority of wars today are intrastate conflicts fought with small arms. And the disturbing news, as reported in the "Child Soldiers Global Report 2008," is that wherever such conflicts take place, many of those fighting are children. Yet how often, when you think of war, do you picture a *child* brandishing an AK-47 assault rifle or a rocket-powered grenade launcher?

At least one such child's story has become widely known: *A Long Way Gone: Memoirs of a Boy Soldier* provides the moving firsthand account of Ishmael Beah's experiences as a child soldier in Sierra Leone *(see "Repercussions of Revenge" and "Ishmael Beah: Hope Springs Eternal")*. Separated from his family when their village was attacked by rebel forces, Beah for a while avoided abduction into the armed conflict that enveloped his country. Eventually, however, hunger and insecurity led him to join the government forces, who compelled him not only to fight against the rebel opposition but to perpetrate acts of extreme violence against innocent civilians along the way.

While Beah's story is shocking, it is certainly not unique. He was just one of an estimated 250,000 boys and girls (according to current UN estimates) taking part in wars around the world at any given time over the last two decades. His book has increased awareness of the plight of children who are prematurely exposed to the harshest and most brutal experiences imaginable, including murder, mutilation and rape.

More than a third of the world's child soldiers, about 120,000 out of 300,000, are from the government armed forces or armed opposition groups of Africa. Algeria, Angola, Burundi, Congo–Brazzaville, the Democratic Republic of Congo, Liberia, Rwanda, Sierra Leone, Sudan and Uganda are where most child soldiers are recruited. In Angola, recruitment of child soldiers is forced around the capital. In Uganda, homeless children are forced to join the army and sent to the Democratic Republic of Congo. Child Soldiers are not all boys, but girls, too. In Ethiopia and Uganda, about a third of the child soldiers are girls.

Abstract

Over years, children have consciously been employed in wars as child soldiers and this has greatly undermined their wellbeing as children. The psychological impacts in particular have been cited to affect the security and productivity of future populations. These threats as they come out in chapter one and two in this study; are a major setback and compromise the very future of the children that various economies are working relentlessly to secure. The study provides an intrinsic evaluation of the psychological effects of war to child soldiers.

With the first chapter bringing out the magnitude of the problem, the second chapter generates further understanding of the causes of the armed conflicts, the impacts of the conflicts, the process of recruitment of child soldiers and the role that they play in that capacity. It comes out clearly that the psychological effects of child soldiering and particularly the associative trauma and post traumatic stress disorder are massive. Additionally, it is ascertained that complete healing can only be achieved if a multi faceted and all inclusive approach that would effectively heal the children's mind, body and soul is assumed. Particularly, the psychological needs of the children that are often ignored need to be addressed. This in depth understanding prepares the reader or the results expected in chapter four and five. As it comes out in chapter three, the study employs primary data to generate the results for analysis and discussion in chapter four.

The analysis of data in chapter four reveals the variance in awareness regarding the causes of the conflict, its impacts and how the same is related to child soldiering. Finally the conclusions and recommendations call for more research and intrinsic focus by major stakeholders, respective administrators and higher institutions of learning to design a more effective approach of ensuring that the overall rights of the children are accorded the required attention. This can only be achieved if cooperation in research, implementation and enforcement of policies is assured. Besides, the conclusion requires further enforcements through policies and legislations in addressing the problem both at the local and international level.

Acknowledgements

This study has been created with the help of my Parents, friends, Archbishop Robert J. Carlson of St. Louis Catholic Archdiocese—Missouri. USA, Bishop Paul J. Swain of Sioux Falls Catholic Diocese—South Dakota USA, my Technician Edward Umberto Adriano (IT Support & PM Pro), who was very instrumental from the beginning to the end. Special reference also goes to my Confreres of the Apostles of Jesus Missionary for Africa and the World, my home Bishop Emeritus Joseph Gasi Abangite and Bishop Eduardo Hiiboro Kussala of Tombua—Yambio Diocese South Sudan, the Adoration Sisters of Perpetual Adoration and of St. Joseph-Sioux falls—USA, were very helpful with all their prayers for my completion of this book.

Finally I also acknowledge all the respondents to the questionnaires used for the study as they determined the ability of the study to generate the recommendations after analysis of the results.

CONTENTS

Chapter One

1.0 INTRODUCTION

1.1 Preamble

An understanding of the issues involved in any research is important to developing a clear picture of the significance of the research and plays a role in ensuring that the research approaches employed are placed in their right context. This chapter presents the methodology, significance and nature of the research with the aim of developing a clear picture of the need for research, how the research will be undertaken and the significance that the study has on existing knowledge and practice within the society as a whole.

1.2 Background to the Study

Conflicts and wars have massive implications on the holistic functioning of the society. They deprive the society of the sustainable health conditions that are elemental for survival and social development. Of great reference however are the far reaching impacts that these situations have on the psychological wellbeing of the society. Traumatic and post traumatic disorders are particularly a common incidence with most survivors enduring lasting multiple traumas that result from injury, torture, physical privation, rape, witnessing torture and death of close family members amongst others (Maggie, 1998). Indeed, Machel (2001) affirms that the devastating implications of conflicts and wars often leave minimal facets of life and livelihoods unscathed.

The undesirable conditions that emerge as a result of armed conflicts and wars including homelessness, traumatic and psychological effects and unemployment usually persist even after various peace treaties have been signed and wars have ceased. It is for this reasons that Weiss and Marmar (1997) note that establishing peaceful conditions calls for multifaceted approaches that would pay particular attention to the psychological implications that seemingly, have long-term effects that have the capacity to compromise the societal stability that is essential for sustainable development.

Numerous clinicians assert that indeed, survivors experience extreme post traumatic conditions that in return have multiple effects on the future generations (Braken et al., 1995; Smith, 1997). In particular, Asukai et al (2002) points out that the inherent violence for children is likely to persist in to the future, further escalating conflict situations. Other psychologically related effects include post traumatic stress disorder, concentration camp syndrome, combat exhaustion syndrome, war neurosis and survivor syndrome (Decker, 1993). Notably, Rapoport (1989) indicates that these disorders are comprised of various symptoms that may range from sleep disturbance, undue fatigue and diminished memory to changes of mood and poor concentration. Primarily, these define the possibility of psychological trauma in patients from diverse cultural backgrounds. However, Smith (1997) points out that; children are the most immensely affected and especially those that are recruited as child soldiers.

Over the last decade, Machel (2001) indicates that incidences of wars have increased significantly and children are being involved as child soldiers. Notably, they are often preferred because of the fact that they are vulnerable and can be manipulated with ease, unlike the adults. Additionally, it is posited that they are easier and cheaper to maintain than the adults (Weiss & Marmar, 1997). Usually, they undergo training, mutilation and they are exposed to drugs that make them unaware of the cruel tasks that they are required to engage in. It is also believed that the drugs give them courage to carry on the tasks assigned. Employment of child soldiers has been identified to be prevalent in ongoing wars in Iraq, Sudan, Sierra Leone, Sri Lanka, Liberia, Afghanistan, Burma and Congo (Braken et al., 1995).

According to statistics, close to two million children are reported to have been killed during different wars and conflicts (Machel, 2001).

Statistics continue to show that close to a million have been orphaned as a result of war. Additionally, more than six million have been permanently disabled or and injured. As a result, studies indicate that more than ten million children around the globe suffered from serious psychological trauma that stems from the effects of war and conflicts that comprise of constant exposure to violence, deprivation of basic needs and requirements including education and recreation and above all, recruitment in to being child soldiers and above all, possibility of being blamed by the entire community for the war. However, the present trend is the most worrying, indicating that globally, close to 250,000 child soldiers are actively engaged in armed conflicts (Smith, 1997). In these, they act as sex slaves, fighters, messengers and cooks amongst others (Machel, 2001). Numerous surveys indicate that armed conflicts affect every aspect of child development (Braken et al., 1995; Dyregrow et al., 2002).

In his study, Smith (1997) indicates that most soldiers suffer from post war effects and their ability to effectively fit in the social system is depended upon proper treatment and rehabilitation. According to clinical records, most war veterans seek medical attention after their return to the country (Asukai et al., 2002). They often find it difficult to effectively transit from scary conditions that characterize the armed conflicts to the ambient conditions in their countries. One war veteran for instance found it difficult to follow traffic rules because in the war torn country, this could result in to an ambush. This illustrates the severity of the psychological effects of war on the soldiers and this could even be worse for children who are relatively more vulnerable (Taiser & Robert, 1999).

Treatment of this basically encompasses psychological therapy that takes different periods of time, depending on the coping capacity of the children. Various humanitarian agencies have set up rehabilitation centers in different areas to respond to these needs. As indicated earlier, the psychological effects are complex and therefore professional help is of essence. These often leave the patients emotionally and psychologically shattered and have the capacity to threaten the safety of various individuals. Post Traumatic Stress Disorder is particularly the most notable condition and its psycho therapy is all inclusive, requiring the affected children to go through comprehensive therapy

(Asukai et al., 2002). This is characterized by retrieving the repressed affect feelings by the aid of the mourning process.

Additionally, Machel (2001) ascertains that the role of the society and family members is very critical for healing to occur. Apart from the financial resources that they provide, the social acceptance that is expected of them is very essential. Essentially, families play the crucial roles of protecting the children and providing for their basic needs for survival. However, during war, families and the overall social structure is disintegrated both physically and emotionally (Anderson, 1991). It is for this reason that Collier (1999) and Smith (1997) point out that recovery should begin by mobilizing the current social system, upon which the family unit is anchored. They explain that families often disown their children once they are ostracized and recruited as child soldiers for fear of being hunted by the militia. Thus psychological therapy is also extended to these families in order to attain a holistic and sustainable healing. The process of rehabilitation consists of three main successive stages of disarmament, demobilization and reintegration (Machel, 2001). Various interventions made at these stages are geared towards reinstating desirable conditions of security and emotional stability that the war deprives of the child soldiers.

In general, Collier (1999) indicates that exposure of children to violent situations like armed conflicts have various implications. It is posited that the problems haunt the children in to adulthood and complete healing does not occur in the absence of professional psychotherapy. Considering the present trends and their implications on the future, it is imperative that professional and effective rehabilitation be provided to the child soldiers for complete healing.

About a third of the world's child soldiers are in Africa. According to a report by the Coalition to Stop the Use of Child Soldiers, a non-governmental alliance that includes Amnesty International and Human Rights Watch, an estimated 300,000 child soldiers, some as young as seven, are actively fighting in 41 countries, with about 120,000 of them in Africa. Another 500,000 children worldwide may be in paramilitary organizations. For those who recruit them, "children are cheap, expendable and easier to condition into fearless killing and unthinking obedience," the report comments.

Sadly wars have been a staple of life since the beginning, they are the battles for freedom, the rise against oppression, but wars are also the force the enslaves and oppresses. Armed conflict has increased in scope an intensity, and the rise one has also seen the continual use of child soldiers, children have recruited for battle in countries such as; Afghanistan, Burundi, Central African Republic, Chad, Colombia, Cote d'Ivoire, the Democratic Republic of Congo (DRC), India, Indonesia, Iraq, Israel and the Occupied Palestinian Territory, Myanmar, Nepal, Philippines, Somalia, Sri Lanka, Sudan, Thailand and Uganda. According to UNICEF estimates, last year alone some 250,000 children served as soldiers, however other NGO's, such as HRW report figures as high as 300,000. Child soldiers continue to be used in Afghanistan, Burundi, Chad, the Central African Republic (CAR), Colombia, the Democratic Republic of the Congo (DRC), Myanmar (Burma), Nepal, the Philippines, Somalia, Sudan, Sri Lanka and Uganda.

1.3 Problem Definition

It can be ascertained that millions of children are often caught up in the war and conflict situations with the most worrying trend being that they are targeted for various reasons. Their recruitment in armies and militias pose various psychological effects considering the fact that in most instances, they are often coerced and forced in to engaging in the same. Even the methods considered 'voluntary' are entirely not so because such children usually run out of options or engage in soldering in order to be protected or get associated benefits like food and protection of their families. Additionally, the training process in itself has diverse psychological implications. In his review, Machel (2001) notes that; most children are killed during the genocide, either directly or because of the adverse effects of hunger and disease that characterize the aftermath of the war. Still, others suffer psychologically in the cruel hands of rapists and the implications of lack of education and other basic requirements of survival.

As indicated earlier, the conflicts occurring in the past decade had far reaching effects on the holistic functioning of the society. In deed, nothing from crops in farmlands to sacred places has been spared in such instances. Of great concern however is the psychological impact to the children that have been continuously caught up in the war. The number of children killed in such instances according to studies has tripled in the recent past, with most of them being maimed, disabled permanently and or seriously injured (Ileen & Guy, 1997). Perhaps countless of those recruited as child soldiers are the ones that have undergone the worst psychological experience because of being forced to constantly witness and participate actively in the horrifying actions.

Various clinicians ascertain that the statistics are quite shocking with the most chilling deduction being that the children are continuously being exposed to the greatest degree of brutality by the same society that is expected to protect them (Asukai et al., 2002). Worse still, the psychological implications of trauma are manifested in later stages of life, greatly undermining the sustainability of the future the society that we are presently nurturing. In this respect, it is posited that in most instances, it even takes a full decade for the implications to come in to light. It is because the devastating memories are repressed and often surface after the war and conflict conditions have eased and the physical survival is guaranteed. Weiss and Marmar (1997) also show that repeated exposure of the child soldiers to traumatic and horrifying experiences of the conflict has long term psychological and developmental effects. It is affirmed that the child soldiers are particularly at risk of experiencing post traumatic stress disorder (PTSD) than their counterparts. This condition is often characterized by various symptoms that include dissociation and withdrawal, unresponsiveness, eating problems, sleeplessness, heartaches, and recurrence of traumatic experiences (Dyregrow et al., 2002).

Additionally, Braken et al. (1989) notes that; the moral implications of war to such children make it difficult for them to be accepted within the society. In particular, it is posited that such children usually experience fear and are comparatively violent than their peers. As such, placing them in social institutions like education centers, without proper professional psychological help is counter productive. Further, Weiss and Marmar (1997) indicate that their goals are oriented to fighting rather than engaging in constructive activities. This makes it difficult for them to lead a normal adult life unarmed and participate in normal social activities like marriage. This failure to function executively is anchored upon their characteristic fear and violence. Psychologists point out that it is often difficult for such children to disengage their lives from violence. Considering the fact that these children are expected to play critical roles in future societies, it is increasingly important for the present society to reconsider the present trend and bring child soldiering to a halt.

1.4 Justification of the Study

Since time in history, Machel (2001) notes that; various agencies that are charged with the responsibility of children recovery during incidences of war have paid undue attention to the physical needs of such children. Rehabilitation centers of child soldiers are no exception because likewise, they lay so much emphasis on treating the physical facets like malnutrition and other associated diseases. This makes the children to dwell in grief for many years without being accorded a chance to experience complete healing of body, soul and mind. Therefore, a paradigm shift in this regard is essential to ensure that the children live a healthy life during the period of post war. In particular, the psychological needs associated with the loss, fear and grief should also be considered in order for the treatment to be sustainable. It is apparent that children in war torn countries do not enjoy their childhood due to the effects of the war. Indeed, the armed conflicts lead to recruitment of the children in to armies and militias, and thus exposing them to violent situations (Krijn & Paul, 1998).

Coupled with the implications of other effects like diseases and disruption of education it is posited that such children are often on the verge of survival. It is because the basic foundations of their survival are usually disrupted. In his study, Smith (1997) points out that the intrinsic psychological issues affecting these children need to be given equal regard. As indicated earlier, experiences of conflict situation have massive adverse impacts on the confidence of such children due to the inherent feelings of fear. Additionally, Weiss and Marmar (1997) indicate that the increased anxiety that the children suffer from because of the war affects their psychological wellbeing. It results in to feelings of hopelessness and depression which affects their development and puts them at a risk of being overly aggressive in future (Pearn, 2003). It is for this reasons that this study believes that by bringing the psychological and traumatic implications of war to child soldiers in to the limelight, the concerned stakeholders will mainstream psychological concerns in the treatment of children.

1.5 Theoretical Framework

This study is anchored upon different theories whose propositions contribute in many ways to the subject under study. They explore the implications of war on the children, the psychological and post traumatic psychological disorder on the children who are increasingly being used as child soldiers. Additionally, the theories intrinsically evaluate the implications of child soldiering and its position in the moral sphere. By exploring these crucial theories, this study was able to have a strong theoretical base upon which to base its assumptions and methodology. Additionally, the theoretical construct was critical in accrediting the purpose of this study.

1.5.1 Pacifist View-point

This perception opposes utilization of war or any form of violence in resolving conflicts because of the diverse and adverse implications that the war has on human welfare. It asserts that al forms of conflicts including the international conflicts should and can be settled in a peaceful manner. It opposes all forms of institutions including government organizations from utilization of force in settling conflicts (Howard, 1992). It is because use of such unprecedented force is likely to culminate in to violence that has the capacity to impact upon human wellbeing. Additionally, it posits that the costs of the war are equally substantial and therefore better ways of resolving conflicts offer the best option.

Further, the theory also opposes use of physical violence in pursuit in any goals or objectives (Howard 1992). Use of force according to this theory can exclusively be employed when the reason for the particular activity is to restore or seek peaceful conditions. Additionally, this proposition affirms that violence can also be used in self defense or in an effort to defend others from the implications of the conflict or war. This view point is based upon moral principals and maintains that activities that promote peaceful conditions are ethically superior to their counterparts and essentially more effective.

Proponents argue that in cases where there are limited options and violence is inevitable, it should be directed at non human objects like buildings or rather expressed symbolically through activities that imply resistance such as pouring red paint to signify blood. This theory contributes to the subject under study by bringing to the fore the implications of the war and employment of violence in conflict situations. Additionally, by indicating that such violence has substantial financial costs as well as non quantifiable human costs; the theory goes a long way in proposing hat war should be avoided in all instances.

1.5.2 Just War Theory

This is a less radical approach to wars and conflicts and studies affirm that its propositions are based on a mixture of various principles drawn from multiple disciplines of theology, philosophy and politics.

The theory was put forward by Marcus Cicero and Thomas Aquinas and generally dictates the mode of behavior during war and conflicts (Jackson, 2009). It posits that it is morally acceptable to go on war when conditions warrant one to and vice versa. Just conditions according to them arise when the war and its implications are capable of harming innocent individuals.

Additionally, the theory indicates that the war should be directed at the enemy rather than innocent citizens and the risks of causing harm to the latter should e weighed before the war is justified (Jackson, 2009). These efforts are entirely geared towards significantly limiting the death of innocent civilians. The theory opposes employment of combatants during war. This provision is important and shuns the unethical trend of recruiting children in armies and militias. Children can also be considered as part of innocent civilians because of their inability to make rational decisions during the war.

1.5.3 Psychoanalytic View

Additionally, from the psychological point of view, Freud indicated that conflicts have far reaching implications on the psychological well being because of heir ability to trigger trauma and post traumatic psychological disorders. He argues that the triggering of the super ego component of the mind makes the persons engaging in war to feel guilty and largely, this is what contributes to incidences of guilt and anxiety (Anthony, 2002). In general, psychoanalysts affirm that conflict situations have adverse implications on the mental wellbeing of human and therefore they are undesirable. They argue that mental health is also largely determined by conflict resolution.

1.5.4 Ethical Theory

Most ethicists argue that war should only be pursued if it culminates in to enhancement of the greatest degree of joy and happiness for the greatest majority of the population (Garbarino, Kostelny & Dubrow, 1991). They argue that incidences that have the capacity to harm humans are morally unacceptable. They also contend that the factors that contribute in any ways to incidences of war like ethnicity, racism and terrorism should be avoided at all costs. This is in line with the prepositions of the consequentialist approach that lays emphasis on the effect of the result of human approach. It maintains that an act is morally right if it enhances the greatest degree of wellness for the greatest majority of the population. Of course incidences of self defense during war and armed conflicts are acceptable by the theories (Farley, 1995). However, the abolitionist thought maintains that war and armed conflicts are immoral and should be avoided.

According to this, any decision or action that affects the wellbeing of humans in any way is unethical and therefore should be avoided. Humans in this respect are central to morality and their good should always be upheld (Krijn & Paul, 1998). Thus it can be ascertained that the moral view point agrees with the propositions of this study; that employing children during war and armed conflicts as child soldiers is immoral and therefore should be shunned. Of great reference is the painful experience that the children are exposed. Of course they are moral beings, with full capacity to differentiate between what is good and what is evil. Therefore, they should be accorded the same regard as other humans. The theory seeks to enhance peaceful conditions that ensure that all human do not live in pain and or fear.

1.5.5 Summary

Generally, it can be ascertained that these theories agree that wars have far reaching implications on the overall wellbeing of children and therefore should be avoided. More benign approaches of highlighting the discontent that the communities are experiencing offer the best sustainable alternatives for conflict resolution. Perhaps the psychological implications of the war are the most adverse, yet inevitable in incidences of conflicts. Morality demands that the pain that humans are exposed to should be minimized. Thus activities that humans engage in should be aimed at enhancing the overall good of the society. The most ideal activities in this regard should have a sole objective of enhancing peaceful conditions. These seemingly would be instrumental in alleviating the pain that culminates from experiencing violence and war. These deductions imply that the society should assume the sole responsibility of taking care of the psychological wellbeing of the children by adopting alternative methods of conflict resolution.

1.6 Research Questions

The following questions aided this study in seeking to address the problem at hand.

What are the main causes of conflicts?

Why are children involved in armed conflicts?

How are children involved in armed conflicts?

What are the impacts of conflicts to the psychological wellbeing of child soldiers?

What treatment and rehabilitation measures are undertaken in albeit to counter the negative implications of conflicts and especially to child soldiers?

1.7 Hypothesis

The Following Hypothesis was developed to aid in addressing the research question

H_0: About 60% of the population thinks conflicts have traumatic impacts on the psychological wellbeing of child soldiers.

H_1: About 30% of the population does not think armed conflicts have traumatic implications on the psychological wellbeing of child soldiers.

1.8 Significance

This study is largely motivated by the need to save the future population from war and violence that has critical implications that threaten the well being of future populations. The present trends affirm that war and conflicts have increased significantly in the recent past. This are attributed to the conflicts that occur as a result of political decision making. Additionally, as natural resources continue to dwindle and the population increases dramatically, such wars are inevitable in future. However, the current studies have indicated that increasingly, children are being recruited in to armies as child soldiers (Machel, 2001). This unethical trend is being assumed partially because of the vulnerability of the children. It is clear that it contravenes the traditional ethical expectations that demand adults to protect the wellbeing of children. Every adult in the modern world affirms that the future is entirely depended on the young generation in very many aspects.

The present trend of recruiting young children in war threatens the very safety of the future populations that the present society is taking massive measures to secure. The psychological implications that include trauma and post traumatic psychological disorders often manifest in the future and have the inherent capacity to undermine the productivity of these generations.

It is posited that by clearly outlining the destructive psychological implications of child soldiering, this study will be used as an eye opener to the concerned policy makers, enforcers and implementers whose decisions shape the well being of societies. To the humanitarian agencies and other institutions that make practical efforts to help in rehabilitation of the child soldiers, this study will provide a framework upon which a sustainable and effective approach to treatment and rehabilitation would be drawn. At this point in time, it is worth noting that timely and effective intervention measures are vital in order to secure the future of young generations.

1.9 Definitions:

The following are the Technical terms hat have been employed in this study

Child Soldiers: This study will adopt the UN's definition that contends that a child soldier is any person under the age of eighteen years who participates in any way in the activities of an armed force in various capacities that include messengers, cooks, porters, sex slaves amongst others.

Post Traumatic Stress Disorder: This refers to the disorder that develops after experiencing situations that are overwhelming, threatens one's safety and leaves the person feeling helpless. It is notable that war and armed conflicts that are characterized by violence and pain are a sure cause of PTSD.

Combatant: According to this study, combatant will be used to refer to any individual who participates actively in the hostilities of war or are conflict.

1.10 Summary

The preliminary or background survey reveals that although various efforts have been undertaken to address the needs of the child soldiers, none has completely achieved the overall goal of enhancing holistic recovery. Besides, the dynamic nature of armed conflicts makes it difficult to alleviate the pain that the children often experience while acting as child soldiers. While the humanitarian agencies take practical steps to provide relief and rehabilitation to these children, the strategies that they employ are far from attaining the efficiency that researchers continue to seek. It is thus evident that there is need for a critical review of the implications of armed conflicts and especially the psychological implications that are characterized by complexity. An in depth analysis is vital to also determine both the practical and theoretical aspects that have been put in place and what should be done to effectively address the areas that are lacking.

Chapter Two

2.0 LITERATURE REVIEW

2.1 Why Armed Conflicts

Armed conflicts and war fare have massive implications on the wellbeing of the society and especially the children that are more vulnerable because of their various incapacities. In deed, the physical and psychological implications of this can be very overwhelming, especially because of the fact that conflicts adversely affect the social structure as well as physical medical facilities that aim at restoring physical and psychological welfare of the population after the war. Seemingly child soldiers endure long term physical and mental effects even in the post war period. It is in this consideration that this chapter presents an intrinsic evaluation of armed conflicts, their implications to the children and especially the child soldiers and the rehabilitation and treatment measures hat are taken to integrate the child soldiers back in t the society.

2.1.1 Scarcity of Natural Resources

The present trends indicate that since historical times, armed conflicts have and will continue to be experienced. In his study, Welch (1993) attributes this to the scarcity of natural resources upon which human survival is depended. In this respect, Sperry (2001) argues that natural resources are vital for human survival and those that have access to unlimited resources not only survive, they also thrive. Thus Smith (1997) posits that the inherent competition experienced at individual, communal, national, regional and global level has the capacity to culminate in to conflicting situations. It is apparent that the super powers attained their admirable status because of their access to wide variety of resources. Likewise, other nations also work towards achieving the same by exploring various resources (Richards, 1995). This exploration in certain incidences lead to the infringement of the rights of other nations which then leads in to war as the other nations take measures to resist. This is well exemplified in countries like Sudan and Columbia where the control of vital resources that include oil, metals and other minerals is highly contested (Smith, 1997). These conflicts, if left unresolved, and when coupled with intensive displacement and impoverishment; have the capacity to significantly affect the children, who in all incidences do not participate in triggering the war.

2.1.2 Ethnicity

In their review, Wallesteem and Sollenberg (1998) note that in the recent past, major wars have also been cause by ethnicity and the related tribalism. This is also related to the political prejudices and mobilization. Welch (1993) points out that in cases when the given society is may be undergoing some form of social change; political leaders take the chance to mobilize the communities against each other, based on ethnic grounds. Collier (1999) shows that ethnicity is a sensitive aspect that largely defines the identity of persons and therefore can intensify the vulnerability of the same to manipulation by the political leaders. This leads to conditions of uncertainty and insecurity that compromise the security of children that are helpless in such incidences. Thus they are often raped and employed in armies. Ethnicity has contributed to genocide episodes in various parts of the world including Rwanda and Kosovo. Walsh (2009) affirms that ethnic diversity in itself is not a cause of armed conflicts; rather it is used by politicians to perpetuate differences amongst the population.

2.1.3 Environmental Degradation

The persistent environmental degradation leads to disintegration of resources that are vital for human survival (Smith, 1997). Soil erosion and loss of biodiversity for instance reduces the economic production that supports the welfare of humans. Decrease in sources of food in particular leads to violence as persons compete over the few resources. Again, children are highly disadvantaged in such instances because they do not have the capacity to protect themselves against the negative implications environmental degradation as well as the effects of the resultant conflicts (Machel, 2001). They hence suffer from nutritional diseases due to shortages in food supplies.

2.1.4 Poverty

Collier (1999) shows that poverty is an independent aspect that creates viable environments for the nurturance of an armed conflict. It results in to situations of social exclusions that increase the gaps between the rich and the poor. Additionally, poor people are deprived of basic needs for survival such as food and shelter. Furthermore, Welch (1993) indicates that poor people are usually humiliated by the society and seemingly, they are neither respected nor accorded the dignity that their rich counterparts enjoy. As such, they harbor painful and hatred conditions that further lead to armed conflicts. Gettman and Stover (1997) also note that poor conditions still persist even after the armed conflicts, essentially because the resources that are expected to be used in social development are employed in protection and other vital mechanisms. Again, Smith (1997) shows that the children that are caught in war and conflict situations are often the most affected because of lack of viable resources to adopt sustainable protective measures. In addition, Keane (1995) indicates that during such incidences, children are usually abducted or prefer to offer their services to the rich in exchange for protection.

Lost Boys of Sudan

When the boys fled Sudan and arrived in Ethiopia they had no identity card, no family, or no education. Fugnido camp, Ethiopia. UNHCR / L. Aström / June 1988

Lost Boys of Sudan

Each Lost Boys has a similar story, they parents were killed during an attack of their village, leading them to begin their extraordinary exodus. At the end of their epic journey, some boys had walked for 2000 km, an equivalent of hiking from Paris to Roma. Itang, Ethiopia. UNHCR / W. Stone / 1991

Lost Boys of Sudan

Two lost boys construct a shelter from branches and a UNHCR plastic sheet in Kakuma camp, Kenya. After the start of Ethiopian civil war, many lost boys were forced to flee a second time and so many returned to Sudan to join the 12 000 other youth in a coordinated exodus to Kenya. UNHCR / B. Press / July 1992

2.1.5 Availability of Small Arms and weapons

In his study, Smith (1997) shows that the availability of small arms and riffles contribute a great deal to war and the subsequent involvement of children. It is posited that the Vietnam War led to massive spread of small arms and guns to the rest of the world. Additionally, Taiser and Robert (1999) show that the low cost of the arms makes them available to a great percentage of the population. Additionally, the small arms that are widely available are lethal too. Security studies also posit that it is easy to learn how to use the arms and children are easily taught how to assemble it as well as aim at people especially those in crowded regions (Ibrahim & Patrick, 1998).

Additionally, it is contended that the global transfer of arms is also complex. In this regard, Smith shows that significant supplies of arms enter different countries each day (1997). This does not reflect the ammunition supplied in the black market that is considered to make the greatest transfers. Dyan et al (2002) attributes this to the decision by the governments to supply the guns at a cheaper price rather than destroy them because the latter is more expensive than the former.

2.1.6 Lust for Power

In his study, Paul (1995) argues that some nations engage in armed conflicts and war because of the need to be considered more powerful than their counterparts. The underlying reasons for Saddam Hussein invading Kuwait according to Bennet (1998) are beyond the need for natural resources like fertile lands and oil. These are the same causes that contributed to the Second World War. Thus it can be ascertained that several countries engage in armed conflict in order to be perceived more powerful by the other countries and the global community in general. Ultimately, power then enables these particular countries to control vital global resources.

2.1.7 Religion

In some instances, UNICEF (2001) points out that religion perpetuates armed conflicts. The persistent war that is fought in the

Middle East for instance can be considered to be perpetuated by religion. Religious ideologies like holy wars of the Muslim community have in most cases been brought to the fore to the contributing significantly to war. The underlying reasons for this are usually morally controversial such that they are geared towards impressing the higher power but at the same time, Eno (1994) argues that they undermine the wellbeing of humankind who plays critical roles in their relations with the higher power.

2.2 Children as Soldiers

As indicated earlier, the alarming trend of involvement of children in armed conflicts is increasing significantly. Machel (2001) affirms that the children are used in different capacities, some as direct soldiers while others engage in supporting roles. These include porters, messengers, spies, cooks and sex slaves amongst others. They are often preferred for various reasons (Adedeji, 1999). To begin with, children are considered cheaper to maintain especially because of the fact that they often stay in bushes. Further, emergent studies show that they are perceived to have more stamina than their adult counterparts who are disregarded because of the fear that they could serve in the armies for shorter periods of time (Elizabeth, 2009; Machel, 2001). This is not beneficial for the rebels whose objective is to derive the most benefits from their recruits. With regard to their material requirements, children comparatively use fewer resources than the adults. Additionally, Walsh (2009) shows that; they are usually preferred because of the fact that they can be easily manipulated. Arguably, children are considered obedient and in most cases do not question the orders that they are given. Thus they can be easily controlled and made to engage in activities that are likely to harm them, as directed by the leaders of the armies and the militias.

Wagner (1999) indicates that the children that come from marginalized backgrounds are more vulnerable to being manipulated than their counterparts. In particular, Machel (2001) points out that the children that are separated from their families are at a higher risk because of lack of any form of protection from the adults and they lack basic needs that are offered in by the soldiers. Also, poverty has been posited as the main cause of the perceived voluntary involvement of children in wars. Clinton et al. (2005) affirms that the children recruited are often under the age of fourteen years although, UNICEF's directive indicate that all persons under the age of eighteen are perceived as children and should therefore refrain from such activities. Although most countries defend the children under the age of eighteen from conscription, UNICEF (2001) indicates that this law is largely defiled and continuously, children are still being employed in these activities.

However, in other war torn countries, UN (1996) shows that the children recruited in these armies do not even know their ages because of lack of adequate registration documents. This is further compounded by the fact that these children do not have basic education. Statistics also show that of the children employed, the greatest percentage is boys although the number of girls recruited is also rising significantly (Smith, 1997).

In Sudan we were distributed to men and I was given to a man who had just killed his woman. I was not given a gun but I helped in the abductions and grabbing of food from the villages. Girls who refused to become prostitutes were killed in front of us. ~ Child Soldier, age 15

Two lost boys of Sudan conflicts.

2.3 The Process of Recruitment

Various authors affirm that the recruitment of child soldiers takes various forms and happens at different times. Most of them are abducted by the militia members and forced to participate in the activities of the armies after training (Maykuth, 1998). Others who are preconceived to join the armies on a voluntary basis are actually forced in to doing it by the gangs in order to protect their families against attacks by the militia men. In instances where the children are illiterate, Wagner (1998) indicates that the recruiters often just guess their ages based on their physical nature. Further, Hinman (2008) shows that; the recruiters target the adolescent boys who commonly work in the informal sector. They are often promised formal employment and then abducted and taken to training camps. Wallesteem and Sollenberg (1998) point out that the children that hail from rich families are not exempted either. They are abducted but usually, their parents buy them out of the camps because they have enough resources. Sperry (2001) shows that most abduction, especially that of children under the age of fourteen takes place after school hours, when the children are heading home.

Further, the urge to join the armies especially by adolescents is attributed to that specific stage of growth. UNICEF (1999) asserts that during this stage of growth, the adolescents usually seek a sense of identity. They wish to acquire a specific sense of societal meaning that would place them in a particular class. This vulnerability makes them to be lured in to joining the gangs. This is particularly common in Lebanon and Sri Lanka where children are in to being trained to suicide bombers (UNICEF, 1999). Likewise, children, being impressionable also join in wars that are meant for national benefit. A classic example in this regard was the involvement of the children in the fight for freedom in South Africa (Michael & Gill, 1998; Rachel, 2000).

Additionally, Welch (1993) indicates that economic reasons independently drive the parents to hand over their children to the recruiters. They then receive financial gain in exchange. These children usually suffer from psychological insecurity, considering the fact that the parents that are expected to protect them are the ones that hand them over to the militia men. However, studies show that such parents often have limited options and are affected greatly by poverty and the associated hunger. Conversely, Smith (1997) and Rachel (2002) contend that some children voluntarily present themselves to the militias and are not forced to join the armies in any way. Notably, this move is driven by several factors that range from social to cultural, political and economic pressures.

In their review, Gettman and Stover (1997) point out that in some instances, all families join the armies and children are forced to go along because this could be the only ways that they could have access to medical care, clothing, regular meals and other basic needs. Furthermore, Machel (2001) shows that some parents often encourage their children and specifically daughters to join the military whenever they fail to get prospective partners for marriage. Additionally, Paul (1995) notes that in many war torn societies, the lives of soldiers could offer better options than other careers. Fundamentally, it is indicated that ownership of guns gives the children some form of power that enables them to have access to numerous resources that their counterparts could not have (Rachel (1999). The public perception in countries like Sierra Leone and Sudan encourages this and children that assume soldiering are considered heroes (Hinman, 2008).

Further, Keane (1995) indicates that some children opt to join the soldiers, often in opposition because of the harassment that they get from the government forces. As a result they resort to owning guns in order to enhance their security. These are often availed by the opposition rivals who are usually in control of numerous guns (Erika, 2000). In this respect, case studies affirm that the children whose parents are either intentionally or unintentionally killed by the government forces often consider joining the rival guns as the only way in which they can hit back to the perceived enemy (UNICEF, 1999). Thus they are recruited in to the training camps and undergo training as soldiers. After training, Smith (1997) posits that they may not necessarily engage in the fighting but at least they would derive their satisfaction from helping the opposition gangs to fight against the government.

2.4 The Role of Children

After recruitment, the children enter the camps in which they are required to undergo training as soldiers. In these they are exposed to similar conditions as the adults and undergo the brutal treatment that the adults are exposed to too. The training as explained by Machel (2001) is often extremely brutal and it includes acts of indoctrination. Initially, Maykuth (1998) affirms that they are exposed to hardship tasks in order to make them adaptable to any environment in future. Thus they are required to carry heavy loads that are often comprised of ammunition. Failure to effectively carry out the activities assigned results in to thorough beatings and in some instances, Machel shows that those that are considered very weak for the training are shot and killed (2001).

Jefremovas (1995) indicates that this violent exposure transforms the children in to violent beings who fail to fit within the society in future. The brutal treatment is adopted in order to instill a sense of guilt and fear in the children. Additionally, Clinton et al. (2005) points out that this leads to feelings of low self esteem hat makes them resort to violent strategies in conflict resolution.

In order to further harden them, Machel (2001) shows that the children are forced to drink human blood and eat internal organs like the liver and hearts of the dead rebels or the persons that have been captured by the rebels. These are killed in heir vicinity and dissected accordingly. In some cases Machel (2001) affirms that children are forced to participate in the same while in others, they are only expected to fry and eat the internal organs.

Additionally, Wagner (1998) indicates that this adult treatment that the children are exposed to makes them vulnerable to death. It is because of their incapability to take care of themselves. In particular, Machel (2001) shows that the training camps are often characterized by unhygienic conditions that make them contact contagious diseases that are otherwise preventable. Further, statistics indicate that these children are likely to die from diseases associated with starvation and nutrition. Since they are ignorant of their rights, Lemarchard (1995) argues that they can not fight for the same. More over, the instable conditions that characterize war torn countries do not give them a chance to express these feelings and they usually keep them as secrets.

Elias Rinaldo Gamboriko, A.J., Ph.D.

Other roles that children play include guarding and acting as spies as messengers. Despite the fact that these roles are less brutal, Machel (2001) shows that they make the children to be suspected by their rivals. For instance, it is posited that in Lebanon, a significant number of children are usually killed by the government forces that suspect them of being spies. They may not necessarily be spies because most of those killed actually belong to the peasant farmers (Stavrou & Roberts, 2000)

The recruited girls according to UNICEF (1999) perform similar jobs as their counterparts. Despite being regularly used as sex slaves, they prepare food and provide nursing services to the wounded rebels. In later stages of their lives, UN (1996) shows that they are usually married off to the leaders of the rebels. This exposes the young girls to the roles that are supposedly expected to be carried out by the women. The rape ordeal affects them and often makes them feel stressed and insecure in the society (Wessles, 1998). In other cases, it is indicated that these young girls are forced to undergo abortion whenever they get pregnant for the rebels. Clinton et al (2005) agrees that their lack of basic skills and inexperience makes them susceptible to intense violence. Since the society is unlikely to fully accept them after the war, it is posited that these children resort to prostitution and engagement in other activities hat are socially unacceptable.

In order to give them the courage to face the acts, Matloff (1997) cites that the children are usually given drugs. This makes them become brave and face all the perceived dangers with ease. The constant and regular exposure of these children to violence makes them less sensitive to violent acts. For instances, Machel (2001) points out that some children are even forced t carry out atrocities to their close family members after they have constantly experienced horrific actions. They usually carry out the activities with ease because after all, they are used to the violence. This approach also aims at making the family members and the society in general to disregard and in some instances disown the children (Bennet, 1998). Thus they become entirely depended on their captors and therefore can be manipulated and used for longer periods of time.

In his study Smith (1997) shows that the children that are recruited in the government forces are also exposed to similar conditions as their counterparts in the rebel forces. It is indicated that in incidences of disobedience, they can be beaten to death or worse still, shot. Numerous authors of whom Ibrahim and Patrick (1998) and Wessles (1997) are represented affirm that a significant percentage of the children have been shot and killed in various countries whenever they tried to escape from training or disobey their seniors during recruitment.

In instances where the child soldiers are captured by the government troops Maykuth (1998) affirms that they are exposed to the same treatment as the rebel soldiers. In particular, they are often abused and taken through the tough procedures that their adult counterparts go through too.

2.5 Impacts of Conflicts to the Children

Children are often vulnerable to very many incidences and war is not an exception. Notably, children are depended on the adults for various physical as well as emotional needs before the war. In particular, they rely on the adults for care, love and empathy. This makes them psychologically secure and enables them to experience healthy physical growth and development. Additionally, Gourivitch (1998) points out that psychological security is essential for any other form of security and ultimate development to be experienced. However, these vital attachments are compromised during wars and conflicts and essentially disrupted (Taiser & Robert, 1999).

In his review, Machel (2001) explains that usually, the parents are either killed or divert their attention to providing security and subsistence for their children. Yet in other situations, the adults themselves undergo depression and stress and pay minimal emotional attention to their children. This has lasting implications on the psychological wellbeing of the children. Smith (1997) shows that this is particularly painful for unaccompanied children that end up as refugees or are recruited as child soldiers. In their reviews, Sperry (2001) and Braken and Celia (1998) indicate that the child soldiers in particular experience intense suffering than the normal children because of the additional psychological torture that they are exposed to.

The impacts of armed conflicts affect all the facets of child development including emotional, physical and mental. Thus Machel (2001) suggests that relief should be all inclusive and should equally cater for the emotional needs of the children. In the past, it is posited that relief efforts have paid undue attention of the physical needs of the children while seemingly ignoring the fundamental emotional implications. Additionally, the psychotherapeutic measures should make the cultural aspects of the children a mainstream factor in order to make the children more responsive and the recovery more sustainable (Eva, 2000; Yusuf, 1997).

2.5.1 Death

Statistics affirm that countless child soldiers loose their lives during war. Some are killed by the rebels while some are shot when fighting (Wagner, 1998). Additionally, since children are used as spies, they are often killed by the government forces or rival groups. This is a common incidence in Latin America. Further, Elizabeth (2009) shows that child soldiers are also used as guides and bomb and mine detectors. Any have been cited to have died when undertaking this duty through mine and bomb blasts.

2.5.2 Physical Injury

Machel (2001) notes that; this has massive economic, emotional, psychological and social implications. Child soldiers often loose certain parts of their bodies like limbs, hands and end up permanently disabled after the war. Additionally, Farley (1995) and Isobel (2000) indicate that others loose their sight and sense of hearing because of being shot or experiencing the dangerous effects of landmine blasts. Often, the limitation of resources makes them wait for lengthy periods of time before they undergo effective medical treatment. This is not only physically painful but psychologically traumatizing (John & Carol, 1999).

2.5.3 Illness and Diseases

Numerous authors affirm that war and conflicts significantly deteriorate the health facilities in a given country and even make it difficult to access them due to increased insecurity. Matloff (1997) points out that child soldiers are usually exposed to poor sanitation, nutrition and housing. Since they essentially live in bushes, access to fundamental health and medical services such as immunization is compromised. This contributes to increases in mortality and exposes them to long term physical pain and suffering.

2.5.4 Socio-cultural losses

Child soldiers usually loose their cultural identity as they engage in war. In his review, Afua (2000) notes that; the society that these children belong to is usually governed by some cultural norms that expect the children to behave in a particular way. David (2000) ascertains that in most cases, the morals that the society practices are primarily derived from its cultural beliefs and practices. Most of the activities that the child soldiers engage in often contravene the cultural expectations. Michael and Gill (1998) indicate that this contributes significantly to their rejection by the society after the war.

Also, as indicated earlier, war destroys the social fabric that is instrumental in nurturing the children and providing guidance during development. In this respect, the families are destroyed, medical infrastructure that provides services to the children is destroyed and schools that provide education and instill desirable values in the children are also in most cases destroyed. This makes the children to grow up unaided, assuming behaviors and unethical values that the society does not approve. Ultimately, Dyan et al (2002) notes that the children do not fit in the society after the armed conflict or war is over.

2.5.5 Moral and Psychological Impacts

The violent and horrific incidences that the child soldiers are exposed to often leave them with lasting spiritual, emotional and psychological scars that may be experienced even for a life time. Keane (1995) shows that the response of the children to traumatic and stressful conditions is highly depended on individual factors like sex, personality, age; societal factors like the degree of social cohesion; cultural aspects including cultural beliefs and practices, nature of the conflict that is defined by the frequency of the conflict as well as the period of exposure to the conflict (Jenny, 1997). The psychological symptoms that characterize these children are wide and varied. They include lack of sleep, anxiety, nightmares, diminished interest in engagement in play and lack of appetite. Welch (1993) also shows that younger children are likely to have difficulties in learning. The adolescents and other older children according to studies undergo a series of stress and depression.

2.5.6 Post Traumatic Stress Disorder

This results from continuous exposure of the child soldiers to traumatic and violent events that include killing people, sexual assault and indoctrination amongst others. Machel (2001) notes that the children that are affected often experience flash backs of the violent incidences hat makes them to live in fear. Additionally, they have nightmares that deprive them of sleep and affect their physical health (Cole & Magne, 1991).

2.5.6.1 Eating Disorder

During the period of war, Walsh (2009) affirms that the child soldiers are usually not fed properly and most of them develop various nutritional disorders and complications. Machel (2001) asserts that they are expected to adapt to incidences of constant starvation. Seemingly, their bodies adapt to this state and changing the trend can prove difficult. Recent surveys in Sudan indicate that the children are even forced to consume their own urine (UNICEF, 1999). The survey does not explain whether this measure is deliberately taken out of desperation for food or not. However, studies indicate that this elucidates their horrifying experiences. This long term exposure makes the children to develop eating disorders and may refuse to eat even after they have been recovered. On the other hand, Smith (1997) notes that others may be overwhelmed by the availability of food and consume great quantities. This leads to development of nutritional disorders too.

2.5.6.2 Adjustment Disorder

Hinman (2008) notes that; this is experienced by the child soldiers due to sudden changes of the environment from the violent to peaceful one. Psychological studies show that this is particularly difficult for the child because it entails changes in personal identities (Braken et al., 1995). They are expected to intrinsically stop behaving as soldiers and behave as civilians. It is further compounded by the fact that the children lost their childhood identity when they took up child soldiering. Additionally, Collier (1999) indicates that the children that opt to take up education find the environments weird and may be behind regarding the education curriculum. According to Walsh (2009), child soldiers often grapple with this disorder and it consumes most of their time.

2.5.6.3 Depression

Braken et al (1995) points out that the children also suffer from depression that is largely contributed to by guilt. They feel that they are not worthy of living anymore because of the shameful acts that the got involved in during the war. Often, they also experience regret and even some seek measures to overcome the same. According to psychological analysts, this is a positive sign because it is a stage of healing that enables the children to realize and accept the wrongs that they committed (Braken et al., 1995; Kaplan, 1996).

2.5.6.4 Personality Disorder

Smith (1997) contends that this is contributed to by constant exposure to violent situations, impressed and queer ideologies and being forced to assume moral ideals that contravene the normal social norms. These children are thought to behave in unnatural ways because of the odd activities that the engage in. Further, this makes them loose the ability to empathize and they become increasingly insensitive to various critical issues. Further, Dyan et al (2002) show that the chronically involve themselves in aggression, violence and other actions that are entirely manipulative. It is because the war makes them place preference to the fellow soldiers as opposed to the family members. Of great harm however the perceived rule of either is supposed to kill or be killed (Hinman, 2008).

Additionally, they exhibit increased anxiety and tend to be aggressive and violent. The cruel acts that the children were forced to perform on their relatives and close friends often leave them with a great sense of guilt that in some instances may even culminate in to suicide. This also makes them be rejected by the society and in most cases; they usually feel isolated and lonely. Machel (2001) also point out that the morality of the child soldiers also changes dramatically and contravenes the societal expectation. In particular, the children are often forced to resort to prostitution in order to cater for their subsistence needs.

This is morally demeaning and David (2000) and Eno (1994) contend that it equally contributes to their rejection by respective societies after the war. Additionally, the society perceives them as out casts because of serving as comforters of the rebels. As such, it becomes increasingly difficult for them to be fully and readily integrate in the society (Elizabeth, 2009). Thus they fail to engage actively normal societal activities. In some instances, this negative perception even makes them be unable to marry and lead normal lives. Of great concern however are the children that assume violent and aggressive characters. Equally, this makes them difficult to fit within the social context of school and other important institutions (Machel, 2001).

Additionally, Wagner (1998) indicates that the long term implication of loss of parents and other close relatives of the children is also a sure source of psychological trauma. Although specific psychological impacts have not been documented, it is posited that they are far reaching. A classic example that shows the extent of the effect and cited by Afua (2000) comprise of the remorse feelings that that various people express during anniversaries of war and other violent and traumatic events. It can be ascertained that the loss affects children even in future because of the expression of deep sorrow and pain during such occasions (Machel, 2001).

Matloff (1997) also points out that prolonged conflict results in to difficulty in identity developed. It is contended that often, adolescence is a stage that gives children a chance to develop various identities, in line with the expectations of the society. Continued distress affects this process because then, the society that the adolescents are expected to look up to for guidance is generally fragmented. The resultant impacts make the children view their future as doomed and find limited interest in development of their identities. Walsh (2009) notes that; this prevents them from making any efforts to seek for any form of help and or support and is further compounded by the fact that the adults that they consider as role models are in themselves missing.

In addition, Sperry (2001) points out that the loss of parents and responsible adults deprives the children of guidance and lack of fundamental role models upon whom they can shape their identities. The subsequent change of the roles makes the adolescents assume the critical task of providing basic care to their siblings (Clampham, 1998). This psychologically affects them since they do not have a chance to enjoy the care and guidance that their counterparts enjoy. Failure to effectively care for their siblings as expected makes them worried about what the society may perceive of them. Continued worry and anxiety according to studies may eventually result in to stress and depression (Welch, 1993).

2.5.6.5 Summary

From the review, it can be ascertained that child soldiering is an activity that threatens the psychological wellbeing of children. It is because of their exposure to situations that are violent and horrifying in nature. It is increasingly important for the concerned policy makers and other stakeholders to ensure that the law is enforced. This will ultimately go a long way in protecting the future generations. Considering the fact that conflict situations are likely to persist in t the future, viable and timely interventions to save the children of this ordeal can only be undertaken by the law enforcers. Failure to do so is likely to have far reaching implications of the holistic security of the society.

2.7 Treatment and Rehabilitation of Child Soldiers

Traditionally, Machel (2001) indicates that intervention measures with regard to treatment and rehabilitation of soldiers has focused entirely on their physical needs. While Sperry (2001) shows that the veteran military suffer from the implications of war, Walsh (2009) points out that many of them fail to seek medical attention because of the associated stigma, shame and the feared loss of jobs. Thus they dwell in isolation and psychological trauma that affects their families and close associates (Alcinda, 1999). It is note worthy that failure to seek medical attention results in to continued psychological insecurity that has long term effects.

The children and especially the child soldiers are not exempted from this and being children, Maykuth (1998) indicates that the severity of the implications is relatively high. Machel (2001) maintains that any efforts and interventions to help the children should put in to consideration critical concerns and ensure that their rights are safeguarded. Additionally, Clinton et al (2005) indicates that in order to have a greater impact, the approaches should also consider the cultural aspects of the life of the children and be flexible enough to accommodate them. Smith (1997) points out that the coping capacity of the children differs considerably and therefore interventions efforts should be tailored to ensure that recuperation is fast and sustainable.

2.8 Rehabilitation of Child Soldiers

United Nations define children as any individual that is under the age of eighteen year old (UNICEF, 1999). Thus strategies to provide rehabilitation services to child children should be aware of this provision and provide equal consideration to the adolescents that are in sometimes overlooked because of their physical wellbeing. Additionally, the definition includes all the child soldiers that engage in various activities and not necessarily those that assume direct fighting. Elizabeth (2009) indicates that rehabilitation efforts consist of three successive stages that include disarmament, demobilization and reintegration. Apparently all these aim at reinstating stable conditions after a conflict or war.

2.8.1 Disarmament

This aims at stripping the child combatants of their weapons. UNICEF (1999) indicates that it is a difficult process especially if their security has not yet been assured. As such, trade in strategies is usually employed. These are relatively effective because they target the economic vulnerability of the combatants. Machel (2001) ascertains that the war usually leads to economic vulnerability of both the combatants and the population. It is because resources that are exploited for economic production are often destroyed. Despite this, conflicts create tensions that do not allow people to exploit the resources effectively. Further, it is indicated that the conflicts destroy markets and may in some instances render the money system of the country worthless (Rachel, 2002). Notably, all these conditions impact negatively on the economic wellbeing of a given population.

Child soldiers boys and girls.

2.8.2 Demobilization

In his study, Welch (1993) indicates that the demobilization camps should be located far away from the conflict centers. Besides providing the right environment for the demobilization process, this far away location avoids incidences of children being abducted and taken back to act as child soldiers. The process is comprised of various activities that are aimed at orienting the ex combatants to the normal way of life (Michael & Gill, 1998). To begin with, they are assembled in given rehabilitation centers and their registration done. This is important because it enables the given agencies to mobilize the required resources that would help them during rehabilitation. After orientation to the DDR program, they are transported to various regions that are in line with their various stages of life. For instance, the children are taken to school and farmers to their farms amongst others (Bracken & Celia, 1998).

Please find attached a kaleidoscope of images of the demobilization of a large number of child soldiers from the rebel army, SPLA, Southern Sudanese Liberation Army. It is unique that such a large number of kids were demobilized during an ongoing conflict. Thirty-five hundred kids spared just another round of a brutal and Machiavellian conflict, from despair and tragedy. And yet, this is only a start. Nearly 9000 kids in South Sudan still bear arms in the different rebel factions, and 300,000 kids still fight wars and insurgencies all over the world, and waiting to be demobilized. waiting to going back to being boys.

45% of the child soldiers were demobilized through the month of February 2001, a figure of 3500 kids from the military contingents in northern Bahr el Ghazal, the front lines of the conflict.

2.8.3 Reintegration

The goal of this stage is to ensure that the ex combatants are empowered in order for them to be assimilated within he society. Specific measures may include availing financial as well as material wealth to them. This enables them to reconstruct their lives in various ways (Elizabeth, 2009). Children are often returned to their respective families and communities. However, challenges arise in incidences where the family is missing as a result of being killed during the war or fleeing the country. Nevertheless, some parents are just reluctant to incorporate their children back in the family setting for security reasons. Often, they argue that the children having spent even years fighting might be a threat to their own security (Sperry, 2001).

Additionally, more stigmatization stems from the community that the children belonged to (Afua, 2000). Some may even want to revenge for cruel acts that the children could have performed against them during the war. The children during this time may feel guilty and ashamed of the activities that they engaged in. In this respect, a study conducted in Southern Sudan in 2006 indicated that most of the children prefer to stay in urban areas amongst the homeless, than risking the potential of being stigmatized by their families and communities (UNICEF, 1999). According to this study, the community conceived these children as a potential security threat when they returned to the communities.

In addition, the spiritual and aspects of the children are also considered during re integration. Children are taken back to their communities and after successful incorporation, open meetings and discussions with the community members and the children are done in order to foster complete reconciliation. Cleansing rituals are also carried out by the community to enhance reunification with their communities (Walsh, 2009). This is important for the children because psychologically, it makes them to be at peace with their higher power. After this, the children are allowed to resume their education too. Wagner (1998) and Sperry (2001) note that they are likely to experience more stigmas in the school environment as likewise; teachers may be concerned about their security. The parents and educators often think that the children might be troublesome in schools and therefore most of them are not accepted back in the institutions.

Hinman (2008) suggests that vocational training needs to be availed to the ex combatants to enable them to economically support themselves. Most communities perceive a male child to be responsible if he is economically stable and therefore can be in position to support a family. Additionally, he is even appreciated more if he contributes back to the community in various ways. It is for this reason that Welch (1993) affirm that occupational training would be mandatory to enable the ex combatants to attain the required skills in order to secure employment.

Further, reintegration needs to incorporate physical and psychological rehabilitation too. Maykuth (1998) affirms that this is often difficult and relatively time consuming because it includes the process of turning the soldiers in to their rightful position as children. Limited resources and malnutrition expose the children to long term pain that is associated with physical trauma, dug addiction, limb amputation and other diseases like HIV and AIDS (Pearn, 2003).

Several authors affirm that the implications of drug use and abuse is particularly alarming (Clinton et al, 2005; Taiser & Robert, 1999; Clapham, 1998). Their exposure to long tem violence and the associated physical pain and withdrawal often makes them resort to drugs as a form of comfort. Additionally, considering the fact that they were exposed to drugs during the war and therefore might be addicted, stopping drug use and abuse might be an enormous task.

For this reason, Rachel (2000) and Dyan et al (2002) affirm that most of the children return to the conflict zones that probably provide them with the drugs.

Post traumatic stress disorder is also a common incidence for these children. This is attributed to the abuse and sexual assault that they are exposed to during the war. Hinman (2008) agrees that their tender age makes them even susceptible to these effects. The pertinent mental scars that haunt the children as a result of exposure to the violent situations make it increasingly difficult to concentrate to their studies in school. Coupled with the inability to solve problems without resorting to violence, the children usually drop out of school (UNICEF, 2001). Failure to acquire quality education as a result of dropping out of school makes the children work in hazardous environments in the informal sector. Seemingly, they are exposed to unsuitable environments for the rest of their lives (Sperry, 2001).

2.9 Treatment of PTSD

Besides social integration that has a psychological healing effect on the children, there are other approaches that can be utilized in conjunction with this in order to attain complete healing that is characterized by wellness of the body, soul and mind (Alcinda, 1999). The overall goal of treatment is to enable the child to break the bonds between trauma and him or her self. The period of healing as indicated earlier is entirely depended on the personality of the children, the period of exposure to the violence and the nature of the violence.

2.9.1 Cognitive and Behavioral Therapy

The method seeks to alter and modify the child's thoughts, beliefs and patterns of behavior (Asukai et al., 2002). The first technique employed in this regard is cognitive therapy that lays emphasis on particular beliefs and thoughts and the undesirable behaviors that they cause. Analysis of these patterns enables the therapists to come up with alternative thinking processes, beliefs and behaviors that are positive and realistic (Eno, 1994). The second method employed is exposure therapy that requires the child to confront the trauma. The exposure is undertaken in a safe environment and under close supervision of the therapist. Continued exposure to these thoughts enables the child to accustom him or herself to the same and eventually, the child is in position to overcome them (Asukai et al., 2002).

2.9.2 Somatic Experiencing

This approach takes advantage and explores the ability of the body to attain individual healing. Unlike the cognitive therapy, it capitalizes on the sensations that the body experiences, rather than the memories and the thoughts of the patient (Asukai et al., 2002). It presumes that concentration on the sensations that the body experiences enables one to gradually and eventually get in touch with the energy and tension that is related to trauma and traumatic events. Then, the person's natural survival instincts from this point take over and releases gently and safely the energy through physical sensation ns like shaking and crying (Decker, 1993).

2.9.3 Eye Movement Desensitization and Reprocessing

This takes advantage of the aspects of cognitive behavioral therapy and eye movements or other forms of rhythmic stimulation. In this regard, the main center of focus is the traumatic memories as well as the related negative beliefs and emotions. This is done while tracking the movement of the therapist's finger with the patients eyes (Asukai et al., 2002). The rhythmic eye movement is believed to unravel the traumatic feelings and emotions that then enable the patient to take measures to resolve them accordingly.

2.9.4 Medical Treatment

UNICEF (1999) indicates that presently, there is no specific medical treatment of post traumatic stress disorder. Thus associated treatment of symptoms such as depression, anxiety and malnutrition should be utilized, alongside psychotherapy.

2.9.5 Group Therapy

The goal of group therapy is to provide encouragement and support to the children (Asukai et al, 2002). This is done by other people who have gone through the ordeal and have managed to come out of it. This provides a sense of comfort and reduces the loneliness that the child might be experiencing. However, other individuals within the group give financial and material support to the child and seemingly, this eases the psychological pain that the child might be experiencing (Hinman, 2008).

2.9.6 Stress Management

Psychologists agree that persistent feelings of stress after experiencing trauma are a common occurrence (Asukai et al., 2002). Thus they are likely to experience anxiety and anger over petty issues. Thus it is imperative for such a child to be put on treatment that emphasizes treatment of stress. The major objective of this is to enable the child to regain stability when experiencing sensations that could be physically overwhelming. Again, this should be administered alongside other therapies as it could not be effective if used singly.

2.9.7 Family Therapy

In her study, Maggie (1998) affirms that post traumatic stress disorder that the child soldier experience can have spill over effects to the family that is charged with the responsibility of providing comfort to these children. Despite this, Isobel (2000) indicates that the family unit having severely been affected by the activities that the child soldier engaged in during the war, might find it difficult to incorporate the child in its structure. For this reason, it is imperative for the family members to undergo therapy too.

Decker (1993) contends that this has the capacity to enable the family members to understand the traumatic experience that the child might be going through. As such, they are likely to provide the best environment for recuperation. Additionally, understanding the experience of the child would enable the family members to re establish the good relations that enhance recovery (Decker, 1993)

2.10 The Role of Spirituality in Treatment and Rehabilitation

Various authors of whom Decker (1993) and Hinman (2008) are represented affirm that most of the wars and armed conflicts that are experienced are usually either directly or indirectly supported by a religion. In many instances, it is ascertained that the faith to pursue the war and the courage to fight relentlessly during the war are partially contributed to by aspects of spirituality. In incidences where morality is contravened especially where the child soldiers are involved, Wilson (1989) agrees that controversies have existed. In his review, Decker (1993) also posits that victory in a given war may be considered as a reward from the higher power while defeat may be considered a punishment by the divine being. The exposure to traumatic incidences during the war culminates in to personal spiritual searching. The combatants in such situations internally grapple with issues of the value of their existence and the overall existence of human kind.

The perceived faith that the higher power is available to constantly respond to the associated feelings of stress, anxiety, fears and the pain that the patient might be experiencing is in most cases shattered and it results in to the inability to effectively resolve the inner worries being experienced. This then leads to an undesirable state of spiritual alienation. Clinical studies affirm that it is characterized by perception of the higher power as being powerless and hence unable to provide the much needed help (Hinman, 2008), the intense feelings that the experiences during the war was virtually a punishment from the higher power (Wilson, 1989) and in extreme cases, a realization that eternal damnation would be the ultimate punishment from the higher power (Decker, 1993). Coupled with the inability to figure out the spirituality of war, spiritual alienation increasingly makes them susceptible to PTSD. It is because they feel helpless as a result of lack of faith in the higher power.

Thus the foremost step that the psychotherapists in this regard should take is to re establish the relationship between the higher power and the child combatant. This can be done by altering the child's thought process and building on the previous beliefs about the higher power. The goals of this process should be to enable the patient to inculcate the spiritual practices of prayer and meditation amongst others in the way of living of these individuals (Decker, 1993). Ultimately, these would enable the patients to give the painful experiences a positive interpretation. Subsequently, they would be in position to resolve the issues with ease and in a hasty manner. Additionally, it would enable the patients to become more resilient to painful experiences and deal with the adversities confidently (Decker, 1993).

2.11 Conclusion

From the review, it can be ascertained that armed conflicts and war have various impacts to the population and particularly to the children. The causes of armed conflicts are intricately connected and therefore it is imperative for the measures to avoid the same to be equally complex. It can be deduced that prevention of conflicts would be instrumental in avoiding the impacts all together. It is also certain that the recruitment of child soldiers is a brutal process that exposes the children to physical and psychological pain. Additionally, the role that the child soldiers play is even more painful. The disintegration of the social fabric that child development depends n in particular compromises the future of the children. This affects the adolescents who at their specific stages of development need role models upon which they can base their identity.

Numerous authors have ascertained hat the present treatment and rehabilitation measures place undue attention on the physical needs of these children. As cited, the emotional needs need to be given equal regard because they have long term effects on the overall functioning of the society in future. Complete re integration can only be achieved if complete healing of the body, soul and mind of the children is assured.

Chapter Three

3.0 METHODOLOGY

3.1 Introduction

An understanding of the methodology is important in developing a study whose findings are acceptable to existing social systems. It is important that the research be designed in a manner that is appreciative of the role played by accuracy in ensuring that the findings of a research are acceptable. A presentation of the methodology that will be used in the study is the main goal of this chapter.

3.2 Research Design

Child soldiers are known to suffer immensely from traumatic and post traumatic stress disorder both during and after the war. The psychological and physical implications of these are massive and as indicated in the literature review, have the capacity to destroy the entire life of a child. The Role played by psycho therapy and post traumatic treatment in the restoration of health in these children can therefore not be undermined and need to be taken in to consideration by major stakeholders. As indicated, psychological needs need to be given equal attention, just like the physical needs provided by relief agencies. It is this knowledge that played an elemental role in adoption of a survey methodology in this study.

Use of quantitative research design was mainly due to the nature of the research questions. Consideration on the research questions showed that they required a descriptive and inferential approach to analysis. Owing to the sensitivity that surrounds the conflict environment, the employment of children as child soldiers and the security issues surrounding the same, a research approach that quantifies the research findings and results was likely to be more effective in developing a concise conclusion; one that borrows and infers from other studies. The use of quantitative research was therefore in line with the nature of the problem and was mainly employed due to its relevance to the research questions. Notably, these were important factors in ensuring that the research methodology was of high levels of accuracy and is relevant to the attainment of research goals.

3.3 Research Method

An understanding of the research approach is important in determining the levels of accuracy that can be attained in any given research (Russell 2005). It is of critical importance that the research methodology employed by any research be reflective of its objectives. This is the main factor that was considered in seeking a survey approach. Use of an approach where primary data is got from the respondents is important in ensuring that the research questions are framed in a manner that is specific to the research problem being dealt with and plays an important role in ensuring high levels of specificity to the issue under discussion.

Trauma and post traumatic implications of child soldiering as an operational factor affects both present and future populations and can be approached from numerous view points. It is apparent that the definition of the research approach is determined by the nature of the research which makes it necessary for the researcher to engage in designing the nature of response. Use of statistical data collection and analysis tools will also play a role in ensuring that the approach is carried out smoothly.

3.4 Research Approach

A number of psychology, sociology and medical related courses in this university offer a topic or a unit on psychological implications of conflicts n children. This fact was got from a review of these courses in this University. The nature of the research questions require knowledge about the trends of armed conflicts and the implications of the same to the soldiers and the children that get caught up in the war. This understanding formed the basis of the approach that was employed in this research. Numerous friends and colleagues taking the above courses helped in completion of the questionnaires.

They summoned their fellow students and their instructors who helped them complete the questionnaires in an effective manner. Implications of conflicts on ones personality being a key issue is one of the most important considerations in designing the curriculum of the identified relative courses. Use of a survey that employed simply designed questionnaires was considered a feasible approach to determining the perception that they had on the study at hand. The results found from the survey were merged and contrasted with those from the literature review to develop an overall picture of post trauma and child soldiering.

3.5 Questionnaire Design

The questionnaire was the main tool used in data analysis and therefore its design played an important role in determining the response rate. It is apparent that the nature of the questionnaire plays an important role and it was imperative to ensure that its content and requirements were understood by respondents. The following are some of the key considerations that were employed in designing the questionnaire:

a) Readability: Though the target population is made up of professionals (students and academicians) who have knowledge on the technical language used in psychology and conflict studies, the language that was used in the study was appreciative of the possibility that most may not have this ability. Simple language construction helped ensure readability of the questions.

b) Time: A learning institution is defined by high levels of activity thus students and lecturers have little time to spare. Only pertinent issues were included in the questionnaire and its length was restricted to at most two pages. This reduced the input that was required of respondents and therefore played a role in providing a suitable condition for high response rates.

c) Structure: A questionnaire as a literary piece is affected by its internal structure mainly the length of the sentences and the level of interconnection between various areas of the questionnaire. Interdependence between the parts of the questionnaires was kept low just as the length of the sentences. The structure was an important variable in determining the levels of understanding that respondents would attain in discerning the content of the questionnaire and was therefore an important variable in ensuring informed consent and accuracy of data collected.

d) Privacy: Privacy is an important factor in determining the level of openness with which a respondent will engage in a research. This factor greatly affects the levels of accuracy that can be attained and was sought by the questionnaire design. Questions relating to personal information are omitted from the questionnaires. This ensured that the subjects freely express their viewpoints.

e) Closed and open Questions: Both open and closed questions were used in the research to ensure pre-set issues were addressed while providing flexibility required for gain of insight on areas in this given study (Trochim & William 2001).

3.6 Population Samples

The target population in this research was identifies as the students and teaching staff in the faculties of Medicine, Sociology and psychology. Their knowledge and understanding of psychological implications of war and conflicts on child soldiers was important in ensuring that data collected was accurate and based on informed synthesis of the variable involved. More over, practical implementation of the required recommendations borrows heavily from theory that the target population was conversant with.

Owing to an extensive internship program that this University offers and the practical experience that its lecturers have, the target population was well versed with the theoretical and practical aspects of the study at hand. All respondents that answered all questions were included in the sampling frame and used in analysis. The inclusion of all respondents in the sampling frame was out of need to improve on the levels of representation of the data and to capture the varied views and thus develop a picture that was representative of what professionals in psychology view as issues involved in the research question.

3.7 Data Collection

Data collection is an integral step in any research that plays a role in determining the levels of accuracy that would be attained. It is imperative that data collection in any study be carried out in a manner that is appreciative of the role it plays in ensuring findings are of high levels of accuracy. The data was collected from students and professionals who are studying or working in the faculties of sociology, medicine and psychology in this university.

3.8 Data Analysis

Analysis of the data assumed a quantitative and qualitative approach and involved other descriptive and inferential analysis. Data was summarized according to the variables presented in the research questions. It is worth noting that under the research approach, it was assumed that the observations made in the sample were reflective of the overall psychological community. Use of the tables and graphs that summarized and represented the data visually aided in the development of a clear picture with regard to the extension of the traumatic implications of child soldiering to the present and future populations. The findings were inferred for the overall population within the defined experimental frame.

3.9 Variables

There were a number of independent as well a depended variable that were investigated by the study. The post traumatic implication of child soldiering was the depended variable that this research was concerned with. It should be acknowledged that independent variables like the causes of conflicts, impact of conflicts, how and why the children are employed in child soldiering and the treatment of trauma and post traumatic stress disorder affect the dependent variable in many ways.

3.10 Ethical Consideration

Security is affected by a large number of factors that affect the values and perception that are developed of the study and its findings. This is one of the factors that played an important role in designing the questionnaire and seeking consent from the tutor. The integrity of the findings was highly dependent on consent form respondents and conformance of the research design to ethical requirements.

By seeking consent from the required authority, taking steps to design a simple and easy to understand questionnaire, informing the respondents on the aim of the research and their right to choose not to engage in the research, guaranteeing the respondent of their anonymity and providing the respondents enough time to respond to the questions, the research design ensured that it is in line with both the legal requirements and social norms. These are important values in determining the integrity of the research and therefore how applicable it is to the challenges that the society is faced with.

3.11 Delimitations and Limitations

There are a number of factors that greatly influenced the scope of the research and choice of a target population. These factors could also affect the breadth of the research and the levels of acceptability that it can attain. They are:

a) It is unlikely for organizations and professionals that are actively engaged in rehabilitation and treatment of child soldiers operations to reveal information regarding the severity of trauma and post traumatic stress disorder that they may be aware of irrespective of guarantee that the information will be kept confidential.

b) Education has in recent times tried to keep in touch with practice and therefore the knowledge and experiences that students and even lecturers have bear close conformance to what is observed in actual practice.

c) The nature of the research questions and their statement in a descriptive and relational manner require an extensive first hand data collection mechanism to effectively address them.

3.12 Validity and Reliability

This research is concerned with ascertaining the extent of psychological implications on the wellbeing of child soldiers and therefore it is affected by the current trends in armed conflicts. These are known to be not only dynamic but also sensitive and therefore have the capacity to affect the validity of the data collected. However, the internal validity of the research can be guaranteed if it is considered that the sample used in the research is basically random and the researcher is not personally involved in selecting who will be involved. Defining the respondents in the research as professional student and academicians aids in ensuring that the respondents are aware of the subject issue thus accuracy. The use of a statistical approach that minimizes the input of a researcher in analysis also plays a role in reducing the levels of bias in the research.

With regard to reliability, the dynamics of war and armed conflicts are depended on very many aspects, with individual governments, several administrators, humanitarian and non profit making organizations as well as the institutions of higher learning playing various and independent roles. The main aim of institutions of higher learning is to develop a clear understanding of theory and even practice that can be used in the various social systems and sectors. It is thus evident that the theory that the students and their lecturers have is what is required for present and future developments in the field of conflicts and psychology. This provides the study findings with high levels of reliability irrespective of the fact that other organizations may be unwilling to provide information for security purposes. More over, armed conflicts and their implications on the child soldiers is a subject that is global in nature which implies that the experiences reported by students and academicians in this university bear close similarity to those experienced in other parts of the world.

3.13 *Questionnaire Development and Testing*

Development of the questionnaires was done guided by the objectives of the study developed in chapter one. Taking into consideration that the sampling population involved the student and staff in the faculties of sociology, medicine and psychology in the university, the researcher designed the questions to be self administered by the respondents. The questionnaire as indicated in appendix1has seven question which were very simplistic to understand.

Besides, the questions were structured to further aid the respondents to in understanding and completing them with minimal ambiguity. Also, the questionnaire did not contain the name of the respondents to enhance openness in their completion. The questionnaires were then delivered to the students and staff in respective faculties through email. Sampling of the study population was done from the contacts of the students and staff in the faculty. By using the on-line system, it was possible to reach more respondents to enhance the validity of the results.

Chapter Four

4.0 RESULTS, ANALYSIS AND DISCUSSION

4.1 Introduction

Presentation of results plays an important role in ensuring that they are easily understood and is an avenue through which research findings can aid in developing a deeper understanding of a problem. Analysis and discussion on the other hand play important roles in ensuring that the research addresses the study questions. This chapter presents the result, analysis and discussions with the sole aim of ensuring that the objectives and the questions that the study seeks are addressed.

4.2 Results

Seven hundred questionnaires were presented to the collection points of which 519 questionnaires were taken by the respondents from the 519 questionnaires that were got only 279 were returned to the collection points. Of the 279 filled questionnaires that were returned 28 were poorly filled and the rest were forwarded for analysis (Illustration 1). The response rate considering the number of questionnaires that were administered and those that were returned is slightly higher than 53.7%.

Variable	Number of Responses	Proportion (%)
Causes of Conflicts	36	4.8
Recruitment of Child Soldiers	129	17.1
Role of Child Soldiers	189	25.1
Psychological Impacts of Child Soldiering	153	20.3
Trauma and PTSD	165	21.9
Treatment	39	5.2
Other impacts of armed conflicts	42	5.6

Table 1: Number of Responses

It is quite clear from Table 1 that the role of children after recruitment in the armies is the most important aspect that respondents consider to have massive implications and risks on the wellbeing of the children. This is followed by the trauma and post traumatic stress disorder that the respondents feel that it undermines the welfare of the children. Other psychological implications and the process of recruitment of the children follow closely with 20.3% and 17.1% of the respondents respectively. On the lower side, the other impacts of conflicts t the children with 5.6% of the respondents is considered a greater risk than causes of conflicts and treatment with 4.8% and 5.2% of the respondent respectively (Table 1).

The aspect on whether trauma and post traumatic stress disorder is a serious health implication led to interesting findings regarding the perceptions that the respondents PTSD. 155 respondents of the respondents were of the view that the implications had adverse effects n the future functioning of the society. This is representative of 61.8% of the respondents while only 38.2% of the respondents were of the view that it did not significantly affect present and future societal functioning. The ratings of the perceptions that respondents have of trauma and PTSD is presented in Table (2):

Rating	Total Number of respondents
5	76
4	79

3	34
2	17
1	45

Table 2: Perception of Statement

The findings clearly show that a majority give the assertion a higher rating though 32.3% of the respondents give the assertion a rating that is less than half which is reflective of their negative perception of the statement.

A look at the findings that have been developed as being representative of the respondents' perceptions of the risks involvement of children in child soldiering shows little difference from their perception the implications of the resultant trauma and post traumatic stress disorder. The results presented are reflective of the close correlation between the ratings and the perceptions of the implications of child soldiering and PTSD on the affected children.

Variables	Ratings					
	1	2	3	4	5	Average
Causes of Conflicts	37	143	19	43	9	2.4
Recruitment of child soldiers	0	35	23	161	32	3.8
Role of child soldiers	10	45	37	134	25	3.5
Psychological Implications of child Soldiering	20	11	54	100	66	3.7
Trauma and PTSD	12	34	36	99	70	3.7
Treatment of PTSD	14	52	21	119	45	3.5
Other Impacts of war and conflicts	101	111	0	45	3	2.1

Table 3: Ratings

It is quite clear from the presentation of the findings that recruitment of child soldiers, the roles that child soldiers play, the psychological implications of child soldiering, treatment of PTSD and incidences of trauma and PTSD are considered key issues that affect child soldiers with average ratings of 3.8, 3.5, 3.7, 3.5 and 3.7 respectively (Table 3). Other implications of war and conflicts are rated lowly by the respondents with respect to having massive implications on child soldiers at an average of 2.1.

There are a few observations that can be made from the review of the results and the picture that they paint on the perception of the respondents. It is quite evident from the observations that the psychological implications of the conflicts to the wellbeing of the child soldiers take precedence over other impacts of wars and conflicts on these children that some respondents have mentioned under the 'other' category. This is an important observation though further synthesis or analysis of the results is required to be able to address issues that are directly related to the areas that the research is concerned with.

4.3 Analysis

The main issues that the research set forth to address are the psychological implications of exposure of child soldiers to the wars and conflicts, effects and manifestation of trauma and PTSD and the intervention measures that rehabilitation and treatment seeks to present. It is evident that an analysis of the results is required to be able to address issues that have been highlighted as being central to the research. The use of averages as an analysis method is employed in research in developing a clear picture of the observations. An analysis of the psychological implications of trauma and PTSD on child soldiers uses both the perceptions that have been developed as the three main risks and the ratings of the risks by the respondent.

This multiple mechanisms is mainly aimed at ensuring accuracy and reducing chance of erroneous entry by ensuring that random errors are randomized thus the research is minimally influenced by external forces. It is important to note that though no formal approach to sampling is employed by the research, analysis employs a basic sampling approach where the respondents involved are representative of the general perception that professionals in e–commerce have of threats that the on–line systems are faced with.

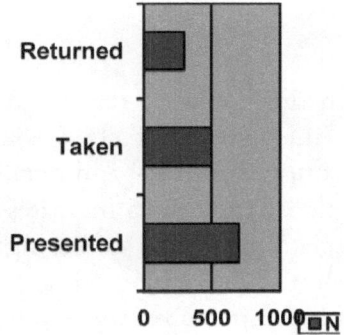

Figure 1: Illustration 1: Questionnaires

There is a considerable difference between the questionnaires taken and those that are returned though response rate is slightly above 53.7%. Owing to the nature of the issues that the research seeks to address and the approach that has been taken it is unlikely that the over 250 respondents involved in the research will not be aware of the psychological implications of child soldiering to he affected children. Moreover, the fact that they are academicians and young professionals qualifies use of data collected by their participation in the study.

4.4 Test of Hypothesis

The test hypothesis designed is aimed at addressing the questions on determining if the population agrees or rejects that child soldiering has far reaching implications on the psychological welfare of the children or not. It is apparent from the findings that many respondents view psychological implications of child soldiering to be far reaching though the significance of the difference cannot be assessed from this. The result from the test of hypothesis shows that $p=1$, x–squared= 148.46, and the significance level is 0.05 (Appendix B). It is thus apparent that $p>0.05$ leads to acceptance of the test condition 'Child soldiering has far reaching implications on the psychological welfare of the affected children'. This effectively implies that the null hypothesis that had been formulated is rejected and a conclusion made to significant proportion of the population thinks that the psychological implications of child soldiering are massive.

4.5 Discussion

It is apparent from the literature review that an understanding of the psychological implications of child soldiering on children though widely being sought in theory and practice is far from being understood. The analysis of the results indicates that the population understands and appreciates that child soldiering is in deed a practice whose implications should be addressed accordingly. The rating indicates that the population perceives the psychological implications of the same to be far more serious than other impacts of the war. Perhaps this can be explained by the increased global relief that places undue emphasis on the physical relief rather than the psychological impacts. This finding is a restatement of findings that have been made by previous researchers that psychological needs of the ex child combatants despite being equally pertinent are widely ignored by the concerned stakeholders.

The failure of the respondents to rate the cause of he conflicts and the physical implications of the same to the child soldiers equally as the psychological implications show that it acknowledges the massive effect of the psychological implications and understands that interventions need to be undertaken in a timely manner in order to save future populations of perceived insecurity. Additionally, they seem to acknowledge that the psychological needs are at the center stage of social productivity and therefore solving them would be instrumental in alleviating secondary effects that are likely to stem from them.

The literature review has explained clearly that the impacts of the causes and other impacts of the conflicts are equally important and intricately connected to the psychological implications of child soldiering. Low appreciation of this indicates that the population is not well informed about the relationship between the causes of the conflicts and the child soldiering practice. Ideally, if the respondents were well versed with the causes and impacts of conflicts and the relationship of this to child soldiering practice, one would expect uniform spread and low variance across the observations. This is not the case for the polarity of the results leads to a high variance that is reflective of lack of awareness or appreciation of the potential of causes of conflicts to lead to child soldiering.

An analysis of the hypothesis reveals that a considerable proportion of the respondents are of the view that psychological impacts of child soldiering that include trauma and PTSD have far reaching implications on the life of the child soldiers. This finding is in line with the postulations that have been made by the researcher about the same.

Chapter Five

4.0 CONCLUSION AND RECOMMENDATIONS

4.1 Introduction

It is apparent from the previous chapter that the study and existing research and theories have developed findings that are relevant to theoretical and practical implementation of treatment and rehabilitation of child soldiers. A summary of the research in distinct, its implications to both practice and theory and recommendation for further studies are presented in this chapter.

4.2 Conclusion

From the analysis, it is clear that the rights of children are often infringed upon when they are employed as child soldiers during wars and conflict situations. It can be ascertained that the present society is still charged with the sole ethical responsibility of protecting the children for the sake of sustainability of future populations. The humanitarian personnel affirm that in deed, the psychological distress that the children experience during war is massive and overwhelming. Even after this knowledge, it is clear that the psychological needs of the children are often overlooked during rehabilitation and treatment. Focus is placed on the physical needs but the children do not get complete healing because usually, their psychological concerns are not addressed.

It can also be ascertained that these children often get caught up in violent situations because of the decisions that are made by the adults. It can not be disputed that children often play a passive role in initiation of conflicts. They are then manipulated by the adults in the capacity of child soldiers and at the end of the day; their needs are not given any consideration during the peace agreements that are geared towards alleviating war and restoring peace. This trend has to stop if the future of the children is to be safeguarded. Of great importance however is the providence of sustainable rehabilitation approaches that would enable the children to attain holistic healing. The following recommendations if adopted would go a long way in effecting this preposition.

4.3 Recommendations

To begin with, efforts should be made by the respective governments and other stakeholders to address the root causes of wars and conflicts. This calls for a global responsibility, especially considering the fact that the effects of the war and conflicts are trans-boundary. Additionally it is notable that most wars are related to the inequitable distribution of natural resources. It is worth noting that the natural resource base is not infinite and therefore, viable measures need to be undertaken to ensure that the rate of exploration does not exceed the rate of restoration. In this respect, alternative resources that are renewable should be employed.

Further, it is notable that re integration of child soldiers can be difficult if children still grapple with poverty and widespread injustice. Primary measures should be geared towards economically empowering families after the war to avoid incidences of fall back. In addition, incidences of injustice after the war should be effectively addressed by relevant stakeholders.

Further, any violations against the children should be reported accordingly. Of great reference is the employment of children as child soldiers. Concerned stakeholders should ensure that the children rights are enforced. Respective governments should take measures to ensure that the persons that violate these provisions are apprehended accordingly. The non profit oriented organizations and other members of the civil society across the globe can be instrumental in ensuring that effective monitoring is done in this regard. An effective approach to accomplish this goal would e to launch a global campaign and enhance the awareness levels across the globe. Notably, the media can play an instrumental role in this regard by exposing to the public the problems that child soldiers encounter and how the same can be prevented.

Additionally, the needs of the children need to be put in to consideration in peace agreements and other demobilization programs. For instance, sufficient resources need to be allocated for rehabilitation programs. Additionally, participation of children in wars needs to be discouraged and stringent measures adopted when dealing with the violators.

The rehabilitation and treatment approaches also need to be all inclusive. In this respect, it is important that the humanitarian personnel undergo professional training about sustainable treatment. Inculcation of psychological treatment in the DDR program would go a long way in enhancing the treatment and aid provided to the child soldiers. Also, the sensitive needs of the adolescents need to be given equal consideration. In this regard, it is imperative for them to be given vocational training that would acquaint them with relevant skills to effectively face life after war. Education would basically enable them to get employment and the resources needed to rebuild their lives after war. Additionally, spirituality as an independent aspect can be very instrumental in initiating and enhancing the healing process. This too should be mainstreamed in the rehabilitation and treatment approaches.

It is also important for providence of education to be at the center stage of government plans and budgets. It is posited that education enables persons to think clearly and relatively, this would be effective in the sense that it would enable the populations to adopt other viable conflict resolution approaches, without necessarily resorting to war and violence. Priority should be accorded in discouragement to engage in armed conflict, prostitution, drug use and abuse and other social ills.

The transfer and use of illegal arms needs t be closely monitored by objective bodies like the international community. It is notable that the availability of arms contributes significantly to their utilization by illegal gangs and militias. In particular, bans of transfer of the arms to conflict areas should be imposed in conjunction with disarmament efforts.

As it has come out in the study, complete re unification of child soldiers and their families in some instances is virtually impossible. This is because the family members might be killed or could have left the country. In such instances, measures need to be undertaken to incorporate the children in to other institutions such as orphanages. Then, resources need to be mobilized to enable these children resume their normal way of life and continue with their education.

Respective governments need to ensure that al children are registered at birth and should take measures to stop possible forced recruitment. This can be achieved if they pay particular attention to the processes through which the children are recruited and take viable intervention measures. Additionally, it calls for monitoring at the grass root level. Measures need to be put in place to ensure that these activities are undertaken.

Further, the concerned stakeholders including administrators, the international community and institutions of higher leaning should undertake widespread research that reflects holistic concerns of child soldiers. This would enable the policy makers, implementers and enforcers to make informed decisions and timely interventions to ensure that the needs of these children are addressed in an effective manner. This information then needs to be disseminated to all segments of the populations so that the children that decide to voluntarily join the militias are also informed about the implications.

Measures should be undertaken to reduce incidences of child abuse during armed conflicts and wars. It is apparent that sexual assault of children results in psychological trauma as well as stress. In particular, the soldiers need to be given adequate training to avoid participating in such ills. Additionally, the emergency interventions need to include measures aimed at reducing these incidences even during rehabilitation. Further, there should be a clear and culturally acceptable way of reporting the sexual assaults that take place during the war. Above all, individuals who engaged in the same should be prosecuted even after the war in order to end the widespread impunity that serves to encourage the malpractice in the society.

The various parties that engage in armed conflict need to take measures to ensure that the health infrastructure that serves the needs of the children is not destroyed during the war or conflict. The perpetrators of the war need to be prosecuted for activities such as destroying health centers, hospitals, clinics that are usually protected by the provisions of the international law. Further, humanitarian aid should take practical steps to ensure that child soldiers have access to basic health care and especially immunization.

4.4 The Way Forward

It is apparent that despite the fact that the adverse effects of the war and armed conflicts to the children have been brought to the fore and measures continue to be taken to counter the effects, the psychological suffering that results from these incidences is intense. In deed, several studies even suggest that the strategies should be undertaken to make the war tolerable for the children and especially those who engage in child soldiering. This is a time for the relevant stakeholders to modify the definition that armed conflicts is given and pronounce the same as a serious global concern that requires particular and timely interventions.

Efforts should be geared towards preventing the problem, rather than taking measures to treat the after math effects. If the much desired peaceful conditions can be devised for a multicultural and equally populous nation like the United States and the overall nations of the European Union, it can still be devised for the global population whose young generations continue to suffer from the effects of war and conflicts. However, achievement of this goal is not easy but still; it would sound cynical to accept the assumption that war is part of human nature. This is a challenge to the various relevant stakeholders that include individual governments, academicians and the civil society community to pool together their resources for this global cause.

5.0 References

Adedeji, A. (ed). (1999). *The Dynamics of Armed Conflicts in Africa*. UK: Zed Books

Afua, D. (2000). *Beyond Individual Needs: Sustainable Rehabilitation*. Oxford: University Press

Alcinda, H. (1999). Integration of Child Soldiers in the Society: Case Study of Sudan. *CODESRIA Bulletin*, 3: 9–13

Anderson, B. (1991). *Communities and Social Stability*. UK: Verso

Anthony, E. (2002). *Conflict Theory and Psychoanalysis*. Duke: University Press

Asukai, N. et al. (2002). Analysis on War: Trauma and PTSD. *US Medical Journal*, 34 (2):243–69

Bennet, W. (1998). Cultural Aspects of Child Soldiering, *Security Studies*, 2: 45–103.

Bracken, P. & Celia, P. (1998). *Trauma, PTSD and Children*. UK: Association of Books.

Braken, P. et al. (1995). The Psychology of War. *Social Science Journal*, 39: 97–122.

Cole, D. & Magne, R. (1991). Child Soldiers: War In Rwanda, Sudan and Sierra Leone. *African Studies*, 3: 16-24

Elias Rinaldo Gamboriko, A.J., Ph.D.

Collier, P. (1999). *Avoiding the Effects of War*. Oxford: University Press

Clapham, C. (1998). *Trends of Armed Conflicts in Africa*. Oxford: University Press.

Clinton, T. et al. (2005). *Spirituality in Rehabilitation and Re integration of War Combatants*. Nashville, Tennesse: Thomas Nelson, Inc

David, V. (2000). *Placing the Girl Child to the Fore: Children and War*. Cambridge: University Press

Decker, R. (1993). PTSD and Religion. *Humanistic Psychology*. 32 (3): 91-220.

Dyregrow, A. et al. (2002). War and Soldiers: Extensive Psychological Effects. *Trauma Stress*, 14: 231-57

Dyan, M. et al. (2002). Characteristics of Persistent Armed Conflicts. *Journal of Peace Psychology*, 7(1): 23-56

Elizabeth, F. The Emerging Needs of Veterans: A Call to Action for the Social Work Profession: *Health and Social Work*; August 2009, Vol. 34 Issue 3, p163, 5

Eno, J. (1994). *Vulnerability of Children During Armed Conflicts*. USA: Human Rights Watch.

Erika, T. (2000). The psychology of War Fare. *Security Studies*, 3: 78-92.

Eva, P. (2000). *Aspects of the Society: Culture, Economy and Environment*. Oxford: University Press

Farley, O. (ed). (1995). *Armed Conflicts and War fare: The Moral Concerns*. UK: Tauris Studies

Garbarino, T., Kostelny, W., & Dubrow, M. (1991). *How Children are Denied Their Childhood Rights During War*. Lexington, MA: Lexington Books

Geltman, P., & Stover, E. (1997). Implications of The Rwandan Genocide on Youth and Children. *American Medical Association,* 276: 20–30

Gourivitch, P. (1998). *Implications of War on Families: Death and Displacement.* New York: Farrar, Straus & Girou

Hinman, L. M. (2008). *Morality: A Multidimensional Approach.* Boston MA: Wadsworth

Howard, Y. (1992). *The Perception of Pacifists.* USA: Herald Press

Ibrahim, A. & Patrick, M. (1998). *War in Sierra Leone.* Oxford: University Press.

Ileen, C. & Guy, S. (1994). *Children and War: How and Why they are Involved.* USA: Clarendon

Isobel, M (2000). *How Illegal Gangs and Militias Affect Children.* Oxford: University Press

Jackson, N. (2009). *Just War Theory.* Accessed, 24th October, 2009 at www.eHow_com.htm

Jefremovas, V. (1995). Cultural Aspects of the Rwandan Genocide: Tutsi and Hutu. *Issue,* 23(2), 28–31

Jenny, K. (1997). *The Legal Construct of Armed Conflicts: The Rights of Children.* USA: Clarendon

John, B. & Carol, P. (1999). *Rwanda Genocide: Contributions and Resolutions.* Howard: University Press

Kaplan, R. (1996). *The Intricate Aspects of War and Viability of Peace.* USA: Vintage Books

Keane, F. (1995). *War: The Experience of Rwanda.* London: Viking

Kiriswa, B. (2002). *Pastoral Counseling in Africa.* Kenya: AMECEA.

Krijn, P. & Paul, R. (1998). *Engaging in War Wisely: What Policy Makers Should Know.* USA: Basic Books

Lemarchand, R. (1995). The Underlying Aspects of Genocide. *Issue,* 23(2), 8-11

Machel, G. (2001). *The Implications of Conflicts on Children.* USA: UNIFEM

Maggie, B. (1998). *Children Concerns During Wars and Armed Conflicts.* UK: UNICEF.

Matloff, J. (1997, January 28). After Genocide: What it Means to Child Soldiers. *Christian Science Monitor,* 89(43), 1

Maykuth, A. (1998). Results of Armed Conflicts: Orphaned Children and their Plight. *Knight-Ridder / Tribune News Service*

Michael, M. & Gill, S. (1998). Child Combatants: Implications. *Journal of peace Psychology.*

Michael, S. (2002). *Policies that Protect Children During Armed Conflicts.* Oxford: University Press

Paul, R. (1995). *Adolescents in War.* UK: Tauris Studies.

Pearn, J. (2003). Armed Conflicts: How Children are Affected. *Child Health,* 36: 162-78.

Rachel, B. (2000). Interventions in Child Soldiering: Approaches and Strategies. *Security Studies,* 1: 67-124

Rachel, B. (1999). *Armed Conflicts and the Rights of Children.* UK: Amnesty International

Rachel, B. (2002). The Role and Implications of Girls During Soldiering. *Stopping Child Soldiers,* 5: 1-67

Rapoport, A. (1989). *Violence: Effects and Prevention*. USA: Paragon House

Richards, P. (1995). *Resources and Armed Conflicts*. Oxford: University Press.

Smith, D. (1997). *Conflict and Peace Environments*. USA: Penguin

Sperry, L. (2001). *Spirituality and Psychological Treatment*. Philadelphia PA: Brunner-Rutledge

Stavrou, S & Robert, S. (2000). *Process of Recruitment of Child Soldiers*. Security Studies, 5: 72-97.

UNICEF. (1999). *Complete Recovery: Psychological Concerns of Child Combatants*. Accessed, 24th October, 2009 at http://www.unicef.org/graca/psychol.htm.

UNICEF (2001). *Protecting the Children for the Future*. UK: UNICEF.

United Nation (1996). *Impact of Armed conflict on children: Report of the expert of the secretary—General, Ms Graca Machel*, (Document A/51/ 306 & Add.1) 8/26/1996, New York

Taiser, M. & Robert, M. (1999). *African Wars: Causes, Impacts and Prevention*. McGill-Queens: University Press.

Trochim, K & William, A. (2001). *Research Methods. 2nd ed*. USA: Irvine

Wagner, M. D. (1998, January-March). All the Bourgmestres men: Making sense of genocide in Rwanda. *Africa Today*, 45, 1, 25-36

Wallesteem, P. & Sollenberg, M. (1998). The Extensive Effects of War. *Journal of Peace Research*, 35:62-78.

Walsh, F. (2009). *Spiritual Resources in Family Therapy (Second ed.)*. USA: Guilford

Weiss, D. & Marmar, C. (1997). *Evaluation of PTSD on Children*. USA: Guilford.

Welch, D. (1993). *Armed Conflicts.* Cambridge: University Press

Wessles, M. (1997). Child soldiers. *Bulletin of the Atomic Scientists*, 53(6), 32-39

Wessels, M. (1998). When Children are Involved in War. *Journal of Peace Research*, 35(5), 635-47

Wilson, J. (1989). *Psychological Distress: The Multifaceted Nature of Recovery*. USA: Brunner.

Yusuf, B. (1997). Facets of Armed Conflicts. *Africa Development*, 6: 36-99

6.0 Appendices

Questionnaire: Psychological Trauma and PTSD / SOLDIERS (CHILD)

Section 1: Armed Conflicts

What are the underlying causes of armed conflicts?

....
....
....
....
....

List five Impacts of armed conflicts.

....
....
....
....
....

Section 2: Children in Conflicts

3) Do you think children are involved in the conflicts? (Tick one)
   Yes   No

If yes, briefly explain how they involved.

....
....
....
....

4) Briefly explain the process of child recruitment.

....
....
....
....

5) What roles do children play as child soldiers?

....
....
....
....
....

Section 3: Conflicts and Psychological Wellbeing of Children

6) How do conflicts impact on the Psychological wellbeing of children?

....
....

7) What intervention measures are currently in place to counter the effects?

....
....
....

Do you think these are effective? (Tick One)
Yes   No

8) If they are not effective, what do you think should be done to improve the same?

....
....
....

9) What rehabilitation and Treatment strategies are presently being undertaken by various bodies to counter the psychological effects of child soldiering?

....
....
....

About The Author

Elias Rinaldo Gamboriko, AJ. Ph.D.

Is a member of the Missionary congregation of the Apostles of Jesus for African and the world (AJ), was ordained in June 20th,1999.

Ph. D (EDD) in Pastoral Community Counseling Psychology School: Argosy University—USA—2012

Ph.D. Philosophy & Theology. Aberdeen University—Idaho USA—2007

M.A—Masters in Spirituality and counseling Psychology. School: Creighton Jesuit University Omaha—Nebraska. USA—2006

Clinical Pastoral Education (CPE) completed 2006. USA

A certified Chaplain: Certified by The National Association of Catholic Chaplains USA

Attended both the Apostles of Jesus Theologicum in Nairobi Kenya and Urbaniana Pontific University receiving (B.A) Bachelor degrees in Theology and Philosophy. 1999

Assignments:

Chaplain Kakuma Refugees Camp Kenya—Africa—1999

Vice—Rector St.Jsephine Bakhita Formation Center/ Seminary Kitale—Kenya 1999-2002.

Rector St.Josephine Bakhita Formation Center/ Seminary Kitale—Kenya 2003

St.Josephine Bakhita Catholic Parish Sioux Falls—USA

Pastor and Assisting in St Joseph Cathedral—Catholic Diocese of Sioux Falls—SD. USA 2004-2012

Chaplain Avera McKennan Hospital Sioux Falls—SD. USA. 2004-2011

On call Chaplain Veteran Association (VA) Hospital Sioux Falls—SD. USA. 2004-2012

On call Chaplain Avera Behavioral Hospital Sioux Falls—SD. USA. 2004-2012

St. Lombard Catholic School—Advisor & teacher Sioux Falls—SD. USA. 2008-2012